The Time-Wealthy Advantage: Accounting Guide

Part of the Time-Wealthy Advantage Series for Entrepreneurs and Business Owners

By Mark Dolfini

Copyright © 2025
All rights reserved.
ISBN: 979-8-9987020-2-0

No part of this publication may be reproduced, stored in a retrieval system, or transmitted by any means – electronic, mechanical, photographic (photocopying), recording, or otherwise – without prior permission in writing from the author. Permission may be sought from https://StrategicBoardroom.com.
Printed in the United States of America

Legal Disclaimer

This book is presented for educational and entertainment purposes. The author and publisher are not offering it as legal, accounting, or other professional services advice. While best efforts have been used in preparing this book, the author and publisher make no representations or warranties of any kind and assume no liabilities of any kind with respect to the accuracy or completeness of the contents and specifically disclaim any implied warranties of use for a particular purpose. Neither the author nor the publisher shall be held liable or responsible to any person or entity with respect to any loss or incidental or consequential damages caused, or alleged to have been caused, directly or indirectly, by the information or programs contained herein. Every business is different and the advice and strategies contained herein may not be suitable for your situation.

Cover Design by Fresh Design, LLC

Table of Contents

Introduction: How to Use this Guide	1
Basic Terms	3
Balance Sheet	7
Income Statement	13
Statement of Cash Flows	19
Aging Reports	23
Cash Basis vs. Accrual Basis Accounting	27
Resources	31

Introduction

If you identify as a "Numbers Person" this guide will be easy-peasy for you. If you're not a numbers person, I can already sense the tension. Maybe you're somewhere in the middle. Regardless of where you land:

Relax… this will be easy like Sunday morning.

This guide is written as a reference on how basic understanding of accounting, as well as some of the more useful metrics you should be tracking. Much of this has been addressed in Chapter 18 of *The Time-Wealthy Advantage*.

I have created a free course for portions of this available on my website. You can find this plus all sorts of other resources at:

https://StrategicBoardroom.com/Money

Don't worry, this guide isn't meant to try to teach you to become an accountant, but merely to have an understanding of what your accountant or bookkeeper is trying to tell you.

Without any further delay, let's get started.

Accounting Function

Basic Terms

Accounts Payable   This is what your company owes to others, such as vendors or suppliers. Also known as A/P, balances owed to others are tracked on the Accounts Payable Aging Report.

Accounts Receivable   This is what your company is owed if you offer credit terms to your customers. Also known as A/R, balances due to your company are tracked on the Accounts Receivable Aging Report.

Asset   This is what you own. Any asset you have will have it's own line item and be listed on your balance sheet at it's current value, unless it's a physical asset like a vehicle, machinery or real estate. In those instances the value listed would be the purchase price.

Balance Sheet   This is one of the more important financial statements as it lists the balances of your Assets, your Liabilities, and your Equity. This shows you the balances at one specific point in time.

Capital Structure   This is the specific distribution of debt and equity that makes up the finances of a company. The entire Capital Structure of a business would be shown on its Balance Sheet.

Chart of Accounts This lists all the line items which show up in your financial statements such as your Balance Sheet and Income Statement. For example, you may have a Checking account at ABC Bank, that will be listed as its own Line Item on the Chart of Accounts.

EBITDA This is an acronym for Earnings Before Interest, Taxes, Depreciation, and Amortization. This is a measure of overall profitability of a business which removes the impact of Capital Structure.

Equity This is what your business is worth on paper if you sold all your assets and paid off all your liabilities. The value of your business may be materially more or less than this number. If you were preparing this for yourself as an individual, this would be known as your Net Worth.

Expenses This is listed on the Income Statement under Revenues. Amounts listed as Expenses are what the business has paid out over the course of the period.

Financial Statements There are many financial statements to be familiar with, however, the more common ones are the Balance Sheet, Income Statement, Statement of Cash Flows, General Ledger, Accounts Receivable Aging, and Accounts Payable Aging.

General Ledger   This is a list of all the transactions which has occurred in your accounting software. When meeting with your accountant, they will normally ask to see this important financial statement.

Income Statement   This is one of the more important financial statements as it lists the amounts which flowed in and out of each line item over a period of time. These are typically run over one week, one month, one quarter, or one year.

Liability   This is what you owe to others. Any money due will have it's own line item and be listed on your balance sheet at its current balance due to others.

Line Item   An individual line on a Balance Sheet or Income Statement is called a Line Item. For example, you may have 3 checking accounts for your business. Each checking account would have its own Line Item.

Net Income   This is listed on the Income Statement, sometimes referred to as the 'Bottom Line' or Profit.

Profit Margin %   Calculated by taking Net Income on the Income Statement / P&L and dividing it by the amount of Total Sales (Revenues). This will be shown as a percentage. For example, For Revenues of $200 and Profit of $10, Profit Margin Percentage would be 5%.

P&L — This form goes by several names: Profit and Loss, P&L, or Income Statement. All of them mean the same thing.

PFS — Known formally as a Personal Financial Statement, this is a form often used by banks to determine the strength of a personal borrower or personal guarantor. They list all of an individual's personal assets and liabilities. The difference between the two is a person's Net Worth. PFS forms are not used for businesses, only for individuals.

Revenues — This is the top line item on the Income Statement / P&L. Amounts listed as Revenues are considered amounts from normal sales activity in the normal course of business. The sale of a business asset, like a truck for example, would not be considered sales activity if the normal activity for the business was installing roofs.

Statement of Cash Flows — This is also known as a Sources and Uses Statement, which shows what is generating the cash in your business, where it is coming from, and where it is going. For example, getting a loan is a Source of Cash, paying off a loan would be a Use of Cash. This is really helpful when determining how funds are being used.

Balance Sheet

The Balance Sheet is one of the most important financials statements for a business owner to come to know and understand. There's no reason to make this more complicated than necessary, and my purpose here is not to make you into an accountant.

Instead, I just want you to be a Business Owner who understands the basics of Accounting. In terms of the basics, here's what you need to know about a Balance Sheet:

The Balance Sheet lists the balances of all the things you own, and the balances you owe to others, at one point in time

That's the crux of it.

So as you look at the Balance Sheet on the next page, you'll see how it's organized into what you Own (Assets) what you Owe to others (Liabilities) and the difference between the two (Equity).

Balance Sheet	January 31st, 2025	
ASSETS		
	Cash	475,881
	Accounts Receivable	844,415
	Inventory	183,335
	Equipment	93,607
	Vehicles	62,222
	Real Estate	1,175,000
	Accumulated Depreciation	(129,873)
	TOTAL ASSETS	**2,704,587**
LIABILITIES		
	Credit Cards	139,035
	Line of Credit	114,257
	Accounts Payable	57,955
	Notes Payable	75,000
	Equipment Loans	24,577
	Vehicle Loans	20,036
	Mortgages	832,784
	TOTAL LIABILITIES	**1,263,644**
EQUITY		
	TOTAL EQUITY	**1,440,943**

Current Assets

Let's pretend this Balance Sheet represents your business. The Balance Sheet is organized with the Assets (what you own) at the top. The most liquid assets, that is, the ones most readily convertible to cash, is at the top. In this case, your Cash of $475,881 is the amount of money in your checking account. But, it could also include cash in savings or money market accounts too.

Your Accounts Receivable is the amount due to your company from your customers for work you've done, or things you've sold them, but they haven't paid you yet. That amount is $844,415. We'll talk more about Accounts Receivable later on in this guide.

Inventory represents the amount you paid for things you plan on selling in the normal course of operations. For example, if you bought $183,335 worth of ice cream you plan to sell, that number would be represented here in Inventory. Up to this point these Assets would be known as Current Assets, or Non-Fixed Assets.

Non-Current Assets

When it comes to Equipment, Vehicles, and Real Estate, these things are known as Fixed Assets – sometimes known as Long Term Assets, or Non-Current Assets. These are Assets you own but not for the purpose of selling, but for the purpose of creating and delivery your product or service. The amount listed on each of these line items is how much you paid for the Asset, this is referred to as the Book Value of an Asset.

Fixed Assets are generally held for at least one year, and are Depreciated over the Useful Life of that Asset. This is why you see a line item called Accumulated Depreciation, which is the total amount of Depreciation Expense that has been taken up to this point in time.

From an income tax perspective, the rules of how you depreciate an asset change all the time, so you need to consult a Tax Accountant to determine what's appropriate.

That's the basics of the Assets. See, that wasn't so bad now was it? Let's talk about the Liabilities.

Current Liabilities

The Liabilities are the balances of what you owe to others. Like with the Assets, we listed the Current Assets first. We will start at what is due more immediate, these are the Current Liabilities.

You owe $139,035 on your Credit Cards, so that is what is listed under that line item. As well as $114,257 on your Line of Credit. You also owe $57,955 in Accounts Payable, which represents the amount you need to pay to your vendors for things like Inventory you purchased, or if you paid a plumber to come unplug a toilet.

Notes Payable is a loan and can be considered either Current or Non-Current. The rule of thumb is if the term of the note is more than 12 months (it is thus, Non-Current), or less than 12 months (therefore, Current). Just be aware your accountant may move a Non-Current Note Payable to Current if the Note becomes due within the 12-month timeframe.

Non-Current Liabilities

The same "12-month" rules apply to Equipment Loans, Vehicle Loans, and even Mortgages. Most often though, these types of loans spend the bulk of their existence as Long Term Liabilities, sometimes called Non-Current Liabilities.

This is it, you've covered the bulk of what you need to know about your Balance Sheet. There's one last thing you need to know, and that is about your Equity.

Equity

Equity is where you measure the value of the company if you sold all the Assets and paid off all the Liabilities. Most companies are worth more than the value of their Equity, since valuations are often done based on a multiple of EBITDA, which is a measure of earnings. If you were to do this for yourself personally, that is, what you owned personally and what you owed, this would be known as your Net Worth.

Although a business is valued using a multiple of EBITDA, this doesn't mean Equity isn't important to keep track of. Many companies, for example, have negative Equity. This means the value of their total Assets is *less* than their total Liabilities.

This is quite common for companies just starting out, but it can also be indicative of companies that are struggling financially. Or if they're not struggling at the moment, they soon could be.

Owner's Draw

Part of the reason for the struggle is how some Owners take money out of the business. Instead of taking a Salary, which shows up on the Income Statement as an Expense, they simply withdraw money out of the business checking account for their personal use. This is known as an Owner's Draw, and it is represented by a reduction in Cash and a reduction in Equity on the Balance Sheet.

There's nothing inherently wrong or illegal about Owner's Draws, but it does have consequences. One of those consequences is that it can be difficult to keep track of how much money you've taken out of the business in any given month. The reason for this is the Owner's Draw line item just keeps a running total, so after a few years it's easy to lose track.

Another consequence of Owner's Draws is it devalues the company by reducing Cash, thereby reducing Equity. Do this often enough, and you can be sitting on a real problem with profitability in your business.

Again, I'm not suggesting that Owner's Draws are bad, but you do need to keep track of how much money is leaving your business.

Coming up:

The Income Statement

Income Statement

The Income Statement goes by several names. Which are:

- Income Statement
- Profit and Loss
- P&L

All of these things mean the same exact thing. For you Accounting purists out there, Income Statement is what it is known as formally. So if you like to feel fancy, feel free to use Income Statement. If you're more of a flip flops and blue jeans kinda person, P&L may suit you better. Regardless, they are all the same thing.

Just like the Balance Sheet, there's one simple thing you need to know about the Income Statement:

The Income Statement lists the amount of Revenues (Sales) you've had and Money you've spent (Expenses) over a given period of time

Income Statement	January 1st - January 31st		
REVENUES			
	Installation	347,679	85.6%
	Service	16,299	4.0%
	Sales	42,105	10.4%
	Misc Sales	-	
	TOTAL REVENUES	**406,083**	100.0%
EXPENSES			
	Administrative	5,816	1.4%
	Depreciation Expense	7,048	1.7%
	Interest Expense	5,679	1.4%
	Mortgage Interest Expense	5,510	1.4%
	Vehicle Maintenance	1,359	0.3%
	Fuel	5,789	1.4%
	Insurance	6,978	1.7%
	Wages	110,604	27.2%
	TOTAL EXPENSES	**148,783**	36.6%
NET INCOME			
	NET INCOME	**257,300**	63.4%

Accounting Function

Revenues

Just like the Balance Sheet is organized into Assets, Liabilities, and Equity, the Income Statement is similarly organized. That is, Revenues, Expenses, and Net Income. Let's start with Revenues.

Revenues represent the amount of your Sales of your products or services. In the example, you see the Total Sales amounts to $406,083 for the month of January. The Sales are broken out between Installation, Service, Sales, and Misc Sales, which is helpful so you can keep track of where most of your money is coming in.

For example, you see that Installation accounts for 85.6% of all your Sales. If Installation has a lower profit margin than Service, which only amounts to 4% of your Total Sales, you can direct your Sales Team to focus on promoting Service. Knowledge like this allows you to be much more strategic in your day-to-day operations.

Expenses

Remember that your Income Statement represents a period of time, and that period of time could be:

- One Day
- One Week
- One Month
- One Quarter
- One Year

This is important to remember since it represents all the activity that went on in your business during that period.

Your Revenues represent what you sold in a period of time, your Expenses represent what you've spent in that same period of time.

In this case, each of the line items represents how much was spent on specific things during the month of January. For example, for things such as paper, paper clips, post-it notes and other office and administrative-related things, $5,816 was spent over the course of the month and charged to the Administrative Expense line item.

Depreciation

In the Balance Sheet section, we discussed Accumulated Depreciation as it relates to Fixed Assets. On the Income Statement, Depreciation Expense for the month is taken to write down the amount of Depreciation and added to the Accumulated Depreciation account on the Balance Sheet.

The amount of Depreciation is based on the expected useful life of the asset, and then deducted based on the appropriate method of depreciation. Examples of depreciation methods are MACRS (Modified Accelerated Cost Recovery Schedule), Straight Line Depreciation, and Double-Declining Balance. Your accountant or bookkeeper can get this set up for you, I'm just mentioning it here so you can familiarize yourself to the different depreciation methods when it comes up.

Interest Expense

The amount of interest you pay on credit cards, lines of credit, notes payable, and other finance charges will be shown here. This won't reflect the full amount of the payment you made, however, it will only reflect the amount of interest you paid.

For example, if your monthly payment on your vehicle loan was $850, but $500 of that was interest, the $350 remaining will *not* be captured in this line item. So what happens to the remaining $350? That $350 amount goes to principal, and reduces the loan balance of the loan on your Balance Sheet by $350. So it's not lost, it just doesn't show up on your Income Statement. Keep in mind, this is true for any principal payments you make to your outstanding loans.

When it comes to your Mortgage Interest, this is usually separated as its own line item on the Income Statement. Just like with the vehicle loan example, it will only capture the amount of interest paid and not the full payment. In the case of a large mortgage, especially as the loan matures, the discrepancy between your monthly payment and the amount paid to interest can be significant. The reason for this is because banks charge most of the interest in the early years of the loan. As the loan amortizes, the amount of interest becomes less and less and the amount paid to principal becomes greater and greater.

Wages

Far and away, this is nearly always the greatest Expense to a company. Employees can be costly. This is why nearly always when a company is struggling you hear of layoffs and downsizing.

However, a business simply cannot exist without its people. It's important to have the best people, willing to grow and expand, who know their jobs, and who have the ability to lead. For these reasons it's important to treat them well and pay them well.

Other Expenses

There are many other expense categories which can be created. For the sake of simplicity I've only shown you a sample of a very basic Income Statement. You can create dozens more expense categories in your business based on your operation.

Net Income

This is the amount of profit you have which is left over from your Revenues have paid the Expenses for the period. In this case, the profit is $257,300 and represents 63.4% of Revenues. The percentage is known as Profit Margin Percentage, sometimes just called Profit Margin.

All the other percentages on the right side are referred to as a Percentage of Sales. These are used as effective comparisons against other periods.

Statement of Cash Flows

A Statement of Cash Flows is a very important financial statement that often gets overlooked. It can show where money is coming in and going out that might not be readily understood by simply looking at the Income Statement or Balance Sheet.

In an attempt to break it down into one concrete definition:

The Statement of Cash Flows combines changes to the Balance Sheet and elements on the Income Statement into one document to show where Cash is coming in and where Cash is exiting the business

The Statement of Cash Flows does this by categorizing three different types of Cash Flow:

- Cash Flow from Operations
- Cash Flow from Investments
- Cash Flow from Financing

Statement of Cash Flows	January 1st - January 31st		
CASH FLOWS FROM OPERATIONS			
Net Income		257,300	
Adjustments to Net Income			
Depreciation		7,048	
(Increase) Decrease in Current Assets			
Accounts Receivable		(42,500)	
Inventory		22,357	
Prepaids		0	
Increase (Decrease) in Current Liabilities			
Accounts Payable		12,750	
NET CASH FROM OPERATIONS			**256,955**
CASH FLOWS FROM INVESTMENTS			
Purchase of Fixed Asset		(170,000)	
Proceeds of Sale of Fixed Asset		2,500	
NET CASH FROM INVESTMENTS			**(167,500)**
CASH FLOWS FROM FINANCING			
Proceeds from Line of Credit		24,257	
Payments to Line of Credit		0	
Proceeds from Long Term Debt		0	
Payments on Long Term Debt		14,259	
NET CASH FROM FINANCING			**38,516**
NET INCREASE (DECREASE) IN CASH			**127,971**
	Beginning Cash Balance		347,910
	Ending Cash Balance		**475,881**

Cash Flow from Operations

The example shown on the adjacent page may look different from other Statements of Cash Flow, but the premise is always going to be the same – How much cash came into the business, and how much cash left the business? This section shows how much cash was generated from Operations.

Keep in mind, it is well beyond the scope of this guide as to how to construct a Statement of Cash Flows, but rather to have a basic understanding of what you're looking at when one is presented to you.

In this section related to Operations, you're looking at the amount that has been generated due to your Net Income, adding back the non-cash deduction of Depreciation, and accounting for any changes to Accounts Receivable, Inventory, and Accounts Payable. The net result of this will show an increase or decrease in the amount of cash generated from Operations activity.

In this example, the result is an increase in Cash from Operations of $256,955 in the month. This will be weighed against the other two items where Cash Flow can be used or created.

Cash Flow from Investments

This section is straightforward, and generally shows results in the increase or decrease in cash from the sale or purchase of fixed assets such as vehicles or equipment. It may also reflect the amount of principal being collected on a loan made by the company.

Cash Flow from Financing

The amount of Cash Flow received from Financing might seem counterintuitive since you're receiving borrowed money, but that does count as Cash Flow on the Statement of Cash Flows. It will reflect money coming into the business.

However, the reverse is also true, in that money you pay on a loan also counts as money going out of the business. This is true if you're paying back money borrowed on a line of credit, the amount purchased on a credit card, or the extra principal on an amortizing loan.

Overall, the Statement of Cash Flows is a very powerful Financial Statement to review periodically with your team. This is massively important so you can see how much money is actually coming into your business and how much is leaving, and what activity is giving you the most benefit and which is the most detrimental.

Aging Reports

Aging reports are simply how old each individual account is on your Accounts Receivable or Accounts Payable, that is, how have they "Aged." These reports are really important to keep track of when managing your Cash Flow. Companies which do not pay attention to their Aging Reports can easily let what is owed to them slip through their fingers, and cause their vendors who do work for them to get pretty upset when they have to call to get paid!

Let's take a look first at the money which is coming in, and that is the Accounts Receivable.

Accounts Receivable Aging

This report shows how much money you are owed by each of your customers, as well as how old some of their invoices are. This will show you how effective your collection activity is, and which customers you might need to lean on a little harder to get paid.

You've heard the phrase, "The squeaky wheel gets the grease." Well, when it comes to collections, you need to be the squeaky wheel. Otherwise, you will get customers that will take their sweet time paying you, and that can be murder on your cash flow.

In this example, you have three Clients: A, B, and C.

Accounts Receivable Aging

	1-30 Days	31-60 Days	61-90 Days	91-120 Days	Over 120
Client A	$41,235	$34,258	$115	$0	$0
Client B	$11,323	$39,459	$23,548	$0	$0
Client C	$0	$12,593	$45,871	$38,439	$5,392

Client A owes you a total of $75,608 made up mostly of invoices between 1 and 60 days old. There is a small balance of $115, and that could be there for a variety of reasons. Perhaps it's a disputed charge, or an oversight on their part, or an accounting error. Regardless, this should be looked into so it doesn't just linger without any sort of resolution. Of course there are many reasons to want to keep a client, but just based on their volume and pay history, Client A looks like a client you should keep.

Client B owes you a total of $74,330 made up mostly of balances between 31 and 90 days old. They don't have anything older than 90 days, but this could be showing they are having some financial difficulties. Client B should be a client you should watch closely and be cautious of extending any further credit until their old balances are paid.

Client C owes you a total of $102,295 and the lion's share of that is between 60 and 120 days old. It looks like they are in significant financial distress. Based on the fact that there are $0 in Accounts Receivable from 1 to 30 days, you have either cut them off from any additional purchases on credit, or they are already out of business. Either way, this should be treated as a top priority or you will likely be looking at a significant financial loss.

Different industries have different risks of course, but the likelihood of collecting on Accounts Receivable that are beyond 90 days drops considerably. This is why you must pay attention to your Accounts Receivable Aging so you don't end up taking a bath if one of your clients doesn't pay you, and you extend them far too much credit.

Accounts Payable Aging

This is the amount you owe to others, and it's really important you monitor and track the Accounts Payable Aging to make sure your vendors are getting paid timely. If you let this get away from you, vendors are going to get cranky and start calling. Rightfully so! You're impacting their ability to pay their own bills and now you become problem they have to manage.

On the next page, I'll show you an example of Accounts Payable which have bills that are unpaid. Just like in the Accounts Receivable Aging, they are grouped in terms of 30, 60, 90, and 120 days.

Accounts Payable Aging

	1-30 Days	31-60 Days	61-90 Days	91-120 Days	Over 120
Vendor A	$21,985	$14,200	$0	$0	$0
Vendor B	$41,323	$459	$5,578	$1,059	$0
Vendor C	$0	$0	$7,675	$27,545	$41,858
Totals	**$63,308**	**$14,659**	**$13,253**	**$28,604**	**$41,858**

In this case, total Accounts Payable $161,682, this would be the amount which shows upon your Balance Sheet.

As far as aging, this is pretty straightforward and much like you were exposed to in the Accounts Receivable Aging. It would a waste of paper and ink to rehash this in detail. But suffice it to say that Vendor A is likely pretty happy with you. Vendor B may have some concerns with you given some outstanding Bills that have not yet been paid. Vendor C has likely cut you off because most of what you owe is older than 60 days. If you haven't yet, you should be expecting to hear from their attorney pretty soon!

There's a lot more to the story than just looking at the numbers on your Balance Sheet. You might see the amount due to the individual Vendors, but without seeing the Aging Reports, you might be missing an important part of the story.

Cash Basis vs. Accrual Basis Accounting

I think it's important for you as a Business Owner to understand the difference between Cash Basis and Accrual Basis accounting. Since the last section was all about managing cash flow, I think this is a good time to explain what the differences are. Let's start with Cash Basis Accounting.

Cash Basis Accounting

The main differences between the two is the timing as to when things should be recorded as Revenue and as an Expense. Cash Basis accounting is usually how most businesses start, especially small businesses. When it comes to Cash Basis Accounting, remember this rule:

Cash Basis Accounting rules record Revenues when Cash is received and records Expenses when money is spent

Let's say you are in the business of painting fences. You go and paint a fence and you get paid $500 for doing it. If the person hands you $500 in cash or check in that moment, Cash Basis Accounting rules would show $500 as having been received as Revenue. This would be true whether or not you have deposited it into your bank account or cashed the check. Simply by receiving the $500 cash or check, you have been paid and Cash Basis Accounting rules would show that as Revenue.

Let's say, however, instead of being paid the $500 immediately I give the person an invoice for $500 and they pay the invoice 15 days later. In this case, I would have an amount Accounts Receivable on my Balance Sheet of $500, and would remain there until it was paid. Cash Basis Accounting rules would not show the Cash In until I received the check 15 days later.

The same rules apply for Expenses. If you went and bought $100 worth of paint at the hardware store to paint the fence, Cash Basis would dictate that the Expense is recorded when you swiped your credit or debit card, or however you paid for the paint at the register.

If, on the other hand, you picked up $100 worth of paint from your hardware store and they invoiced you, under Cash Basis rules the Expense would not show up as an Expense until you paid the invoice at a later date. Writing a check would be considered "paying" the invoice.

Most businesses are fine to use Cash Basis and stay with Cash Basis. It's cheaper, and usually much easier for people to understand. However, there are reasons to use Accrual Basis Accounting. Let's start by describing what that is.

Accrual Basis Accounting

Like I said earlier, the main difference between Cash and Accrual basis is timing. While Cash Basis Accounting records a Revenue once cash is received and when money is spent, Accrual Basis Accounting looks at things a little differently. When it comes to Accrual Basis Accounting, remember this rule:

Accrual Basis Accounting rules record Revenues when money is earned and Expenses when they are incurred

To explain this, let's go back to our painting business example. Once you painted the fence, Accrual Basis rules would consider that as Revenue since the performance of your work has been completed. This is true whether or not the person handed you money at the end of the job.

Expenses follow a similar ideology. In the case of buying paint, you would record the Expense when you purchased the paint and walked out of the store with it, regardless of when you actually paid for it.

Why Use Accrual Basis Accounting?

Accrual Basis Accounting sounds more complicated, and it is a little, but not terribly so. But why use it at all? There are reasons dictated by the IRS which involves certain types of businesses and businesses of a certain size. For example, the IRS requires C-Corps over a certain amount of revenue to use Accrual Accounting, as well as certain tax shelters. These rules evolve all the time, so I won't get into the weeds on this here, but the IRS does have a hand in how certain businesses report their Revenues and Expenses.

There is a benefit, however, to using Accrual Basis. This is especially true if the business has a large amount of Accounts Receivable and Accounts Payable. The reason for this is because of a concept called Matching.

Since both Revenues and Expenses are recorded in the month earned and incurred, this helps to match the Revenue to the Expenses it took to deliver that to the customer in the same time period.

For example, let's say you had 50 crews of fence painters and you painted 500 fences in a month but you didn't get paid for any of them. That would make your month look horrible under Cash Basis since you'd have a lot of Expenses in the way of paint and wages, but since you didn't get paid you would not report any Revenues. In this case, Cash Basis would show you a very skewed view of what's actually going on in your business.

Accrual Basis allows you to match the Revenues in the month when jobs are completed to the Expenses related to that job and incurred in the same month. So in this case, Accrual Basis gives a much more accurate financial picture as to what's going on in the business.

Resources

Looking for more? There's a lot more where this came from. Just head over to the main website for more resources, some free, some cost a few dollars, but if you found value here you'll surely find more there.

https://StrategicBoardroom.com/Money

Made in the USA
Monee, IL
01 June 2025